ENTER THE DOJO!

MARTIAL ARTS FOR KIDS

KARATE

AMANDA VINK

PowerKiDS
press

New York

Published in 2020 by The Rosen Publishing Group, Inc.
29 East 21st Street, New York, NY 10010

First Edition

Editor: Greg Roza
Book Design: Reann Nye

Photo Credits: Series art Reinhold Leitner/Shutterstock.com; cover Icon Sport/Getty Images; p. 5 7stock/Shutterstock.com; p. 7 DEUTSCH Jean-Claude/GYSEMBERGH Benoit/Paris Match Archive/Getty Images; p. 8 Ljupco Smokovski/Shutterstock.com; p. 9 Ianarta/Shutterstock.com; p. 11 Adrian Green/The Image Bank/Getty Images Plus/Getty Images; p. 12 Jade ThaiCatwalk/Shutterstock.com; p. 13 Satyrenko/Shutterstock.com; p. 14 Master1305/Shutterstock.com; pp. 15, 19 Dave Winter/Icon Iakov Filimonov Sport/Getty Images; p. 17 Iakov Filimonov/Shutterstock.com; p. 21 emyerson/E+/Getty Images; p. 22 Lucian Coman/Shutterstock.com.

Cataloging-in-Publication Data

Names: Vink, Amanda.
Title: Karate / Amanda Vink.
Description: New York : PowerKids Press, 2020. | Series: Enter the dojo! martial arts for kids | Includes glossary and index.
Identifiers: ISBN 9781725310148 (pbk.) | ISBN 9781725310162 (library bound) | ISBN 9781725310155 (6 pack)
Subjects: LCSH: Karate–Juvenile literature.
Classification: LCC GV1114.3 V56 2020 | DDC 796.815'3–dc23

Manufactured in the United States of America

The activities discussed and displayed in this book can cause serious injury when attempted by someone who is untrained in the martial arts. Never try to replicate the techniques in this book without the supervision of a trained martial arts instructor.

CPSIA Compliance Information: Batch #CWPK20. For Further Information contact Rosen Publishing, New York, New York at 1-800-237-9932.

CONTENTS

Empty Hands

Karate is one of the most popular types of martial arts practiced worldwide! It's also an effective method of self-defense. Compared to other martial arts, karate focuses on strikes, such as punching, kicking, and open-handed attacks. Students of karate, called "karateka," **dedicate** themselves to both physical movement and mental control. "Karate" means "empty hand." This shows karate's focus on unarmed **combat**.

Karate is a fun martial art to practice. It's also a lot of work. Becoming a master of karate can take many years—and even masters of karate continue to learn!

Kiai!

Many karatekas feel that karate training guides different parts of their lives and makes them better people. They live by the idea of "karate-do," or the "empty hand way."

It doesn't matter how old you are.
Anyone can enjoy karate!

5

The History of Karate

Karate was created in Okinawa, Japan, in the 17th century. The military leader of Japan outlawed weapons around 1609, so Okinawans created karate in secret. This early form—based on an ancient style of kung fu—was used as self-defense against **samurai**.

In the late 19th century, Japanese culture began to change. The laws against martial arts were removed. Now people could practice karate in the open. Still, karate masters chose to keep the skills to themselves. During World War II, American troops occupied Okinawa, Japan. Karate instructors began training American soldiers. Many American servicemen brought the art back to America after the war.

Kiai!

Karate became more well-known in 1922 after Gichin Funakoshi gave a karate show in Tokyo. Funakoshi created the karate style Shotokan and is known as the father of modern karate.

American Chuck Norris joined the U.S. Air Force in 1958, and he served in Korea during the Korean War. He learned karate during that time. Later, Norris opened many dojos in the United States, and he went on to become an action movie superstar.

Inside the Dojo

A dojo is a school where karatekas practice karate. To find a dojo, it may be a good idea to find out which schools near you are connected to a major karate organization.

Kiai!

Bowing is a sign of respect in the martial arts. Most dojos require that a student bows upon entering the space. Many dojos ask students to bow to a picture of the style's founders when entering the dojo. Also, students are expected to bow to one another and to instructors throughout practice.

Even though karate means "empty hand," training with basic weapons is an important part of karate. The first weapon most students train with is the bo, also called the bo staff.

A karateka wears a gi, or a uniform, and is usually barefoot within the dojo. Sometimes students are required to buy equipment, such as mouthguards and padded gloves. Later, a student may begin to train with weapons, many of which are inspired by Okinawan farming equipment. Examples include the tonfa, based on a handle for a **millstone**, and the kama, a small handheld blade used for collecting crops.

Mindset

Karate is not meant to start fights. In **traditional** karate training, a karateka seeks to improve their character. The martial art, which requires a balance of mind and body, is taught to be used in self-defense and for **competition**.

The Kenpo **Creed** has become a code of ethics, or beliefs, for many karate students. Part of it reads: "I have no weapons, but should I be forced to defend myself, my principles or my honor, should it be a matter of life or death, of right or wrong, then here are my weapons: karate, my empty hands."

American martial artist Ed Parker created modern Kenpo, which is based on a traditional karate style. Parker's style took shape between 1954 and 1990 and is sometimes called American Kenpo or Parker Kenpo.

Katas

Karate students learn katas, which is Japanese for "forms." These movements are practiced to build muscle memory, which is when a person no longer has to think about the movements. Katas show different types of attacks. Katas use different stances, or ways of standing, and they help karatekas learn how to move from one stance to another. Some karatekas use katas as a form of **meditation**.

Kiai!

Different forms of karate have different katas. However, some katas can be found in many different kinds of karate. For example, most karate students learn a form of Seisan kata, regardless of the type of karate they are studying.

Karatekas practice katas as a class. Individuals often need to perform katas alone in front of judges in order to move up to the next level.

Most katas are very old and were created with a particular purpose. For example, a well-constructed kata may teach students about balance. Another may focus on a particular stance. Yet another may feature different kinds of hand strikes.

Strikes and Kicks

In karate, karatekas use all parts of the hand to strike. The most popular strike is a straight punch, called the seiken. The back of the fist, called the uraken, is often used to strike a rival's head and face. In time, martial artists create enough power to break wooden boards! Some masters even break bricks with their bare hands.

Kiai!

Karatekas often yell "kiai!" (or something similar) while striking. This "spirited shout" is not just for show. It helps the karateka create more power and helps them breathe properly during a match.

14

To do a roundhouse kick, the karateka spins their hips in the direction of the kick, and then snaps their leg out straight. This creates a lot of power.

Students of karate learn to kick from the front, the side, and the back. One memorable kick is called a roundhouse kick, or the mawashi-geri. This powerful kick uses the motion of the hips, and it's useful for knocking an **opponent** off-balance.

Sparring

Two or more karatekas practice their fighting skills by going against each other in an arranged fight called sparring, or kumite. Certain drills are practiced in sparring until they become second nature. Some schools use padding during sparring, but this is also an opportunity for a student to practice blocking attacks.

Some karate dojos have begun to teach mixed martial arts (MMA) **techniques**, such as grappling. Grappling takes place on the ground. Karate students often learn the basics of other martial arts, particularly judo, jujitsu, and Brazilian jujitsu. When practiced together, these martial arts help make the karateka a well-rounded martial artist.

Kiai!

Many karate dojos are considered mixed martial arts schools, meaning students learn more than just karate skills.

During sparring, a karateka may be asked to "go 50 percent" instead of trying their hardest. This is to help less-experienced students learn the basic techniques and to avoid injuries.

Competitive Karate

Many karatekas move outside of their home dojos in order to join competitions. Many competitions feature kata performances, while others **evaluate** sparring matches for points. Judges watch for speed, strength, balance, and knowledge of karate skills. The World Karate Federation holds the Karate World Championships every two years in different cities around the world. The first championship was held in 1970 in Tokyo, Japan. Tokyo hosted again in 1977 and 2008. In 2020, the competition was held in Dubai, United Arab Emirates.

In 2020, karate was finally honored as an official sport of the Olympics in Tokyo. Both men and women competed in sparring and kata events.

Kiai!

In addition to karate competitions, many karate students choose to become professional MMA fighters once they've trained for many years. Professional means they do it for a living.

19

Moving Up

Karate students advance through a series of colored belts as they improve. These belts stand for levels of experience and skill, or kyus. Often the colors in karate are awarded as follows: white, yellow, orange, green, blue, purple, brown, and black. There are often multiple levels (called stripes) for each of the colored belts.

While becoming a black belt is a very exciting step, it does not mean the end of training. Earning a black belt, called the first dan, means that one has mastered the basics of karate. Every level up after that is a new dan.

Kiai!

To move up in belt color, a student must pass a test that follows the dojo's **curriculum**. Different styles of karate focus on different techniques and katas. Many dojos also expect students to pass a written test.

Black belts are referred to as "sensei" when they are wearing their black belts. This is Japanese for "teacher." A "shihan" is a master teacher.

21

The Karate Community

Joining a karate dojo is a lot of work, but it's also a lot of fun! By training as a karateka, you will have the opportunity to become faster and stronger, both in body and in mind. You also can become part of the karate community, who will support you in your journey to becoming a black belt and beyond.

You may wish someday to become an instructor of karate. There is a separate system in karate dojos that trains people to teach others. No matter what your interests, there is a karate path for you. Are you ready to enter the dojo?

GLOSSARY

combat: A fight or contest between people or groups.

competition: The act or process of trying to win a contest others are also trying to win. Also, the contest itself.

creed: A set of beliefs or a guiding principle.

curriculum: All the courses of study offered by a school.

dedicate: To commit to a goal.

evaluate: To judge the value or condition of (someone or something) in a careful and thoughtful way.

meditation: The act or process of spending time in quiet thought.

millstone: Either of two circular stones used for grinding something, such as grain.

opponent: Someone competing against another person.

samurai: A highly trained soldier of the Japanese military class in the past.

technique: The manner in which physical movements are used for a particular purpose, such as training in a martial art.

traditional: Handed down from age to age.

INDEX

WEBSITES

Due to the changing nature of Internet links, PowerKids Press has developed an online list of websites related to the subject of this book. This site is updated regularly. Please use this link to access the list: www.powerkidslinks.com/ETD/karate